HOW
ON
EARTH
DO
WE
RECYCLE
PAPER?

HOW ON EARTH DO WE RECYCLE

PAPER?

HELEN JILL FLETCHER
and
SELI GROVES

Illustrations by

ART SEIDEN

THE MILLBROOK PRESS
Brookfield, Connecticut

The photos are courtesy of
the American Paper Institute, pp. 6, 14, 15, 21, 23;
The New York Public Library, p. 9;
Bulkley Dunton, p. 11;
Scott Paper Co., p. 13;
City of New York Sanitation Dept., p. 17;
The Paper Bag Players and Martha Swope, p. 19, and Ken Howard, p. 38;
Jerry Telfer and San Francisco Chronicle, p. 25.

Produced in association with **STEARN/KNUDSEN & CO.**

Printed in the United States of America
5 4 3 2 1

Library of Congress Cataloging-in-Publication Data
Fletcher, Helen Jill.
How on earth do we recycle paper? / by Helen Jill Fletcher and Seli Groves;
illustrated by Art Seiden.
p.   cm.
Includes bibliographical references and index.
Summary: Discusses how paper is produced and how it is recycled. Presents
crafts projects using paper discards.
ISBN 1-56294-140-2
1. Waste paper — Recycling — Juvenile literature. 2. Paper work — Juvenile
literature . [1. Waste paper — Recycling. 2. Recycling (Waste) 3. Paper work.
4. Handicraft.] I. Groves, Seli. II. Seiden, Art, ill. III. Title.
TD805.F54 1992
676'.142—dc20
91-24404 CIP AC

This book is printed on recycled paper.

CONTENTS

The first recycled paper in America was made in the early 1700s at the Rittenhouse Mill near Philadelphia.

1 HOW ON EARTH DO WE RECYCLE PAPER?

Ideas on Paper

Paper is a fiber product. Whether it's made of wood chips, tree bark, flax, rags, or hemp, its basic ingredient—the stuff that makes it paper—is cellulose, or plant fiber. This material is related to the dietary fibers in fruits and vegetables that doctors say are essential for our good health.

Paper is essential for the good health of the world's economy, too. Without paper, many of the industries and products we take for granted simply wouldn't exist. Although paper may not seem to be part of such products as your family's washing machine or waffle iron, or your violin or soccer ball, it is part of the process that transforms these objects from a concept into a finished product.

You see, every product starts as an idea that is developed into a plan and then reproduced on paper. For example, a pattern is made for a dress, a design is drawn for an automobile, or a blueprint for a building. Even this book started as an idea, which was followed by an outline of what would be in the final manuscript. The designs made on computers are printed out on paper, as well.

Paper is the basic material we use for written communication. On paper, we are able to pass knowledge from one generation to the next. There's no doubt about it: without paper, the world would be very different from what it is today.

A list of all the things that are made of paper and that paper helps make is too long to include here. But to cite a few—there are paper dollars and paper dolls, paper bags and paper rags, paper towels and paper tissues, as well as newspapers, which require tons of paper for each daily issue. We write on it, type on it, and paint watercolors on it. We wrap with it and pack with it. We can make paper trays out of papier-mâché. And, thanks to recycling, we can take paper, which was made from logs, and make new, artificial logs, which people use as fuel. There are a hundreds of uses for paper, and they keep increasing all the time.

The First Papermakers

Before paper was invented, people put symbols on many materials to communicate their ideas and stories. Some of our ancestors painted pictures on the walls of caves. An ancient people called the Sumerians (who lived in an area of what is now Iraq) wrote letters and kept their household accounts on wet clay tablets by etching symbols into the clay with a stylus, or pointed stick. The clay was then baked into hardened tablets that could be sent to others by messenger. Although clay tablets didn't yellow, flake, or fade like some types of paper do, filing them must have been difficult. And, can you imagine being a Sumerian postal worker toting a heavy pack of tablets on your daily rounds!

People also wrote on animal skins—the best came from sheep and goats. These skins were dried out to create a material called parchment. People continue to use parchment for bookbindings, drums, and for special documents. The Old Testament of the Bible, the sacred book Jews call the Torah, is still written on parchment. Until recently, colleges and universities awarded parchment diplomas, which is why graduates say they received a "sheepskin."

The biggest breakthrough in writing materials took place in Egypt thousands of years ago when vegetable fibers were first used to make a new writing material called papyrus. The Egyptians used the papyrus reed growing along the Nile River to fulfill many of their daily needs: they burned the roots for fuel; they ate the pith, or fruit; and they wove the stems into sandals, mats, boxes, twine, cloth, and sails. They also pressed it into a writing material, which, too, was called papyrus.

Before the invention of paper, Egyptians wrote on papyrus.

Nature's Papermakers. Paper, as we know it, was invented in China in the year 105 A.D. Chinese history credits the invention to a man named Ts'ai Lun, an official who worked for the emperor.

A story about Ts'ai Lun relates how he may have got the idea for making paper. As a little boy, he liked to watch wasps build their nests in his family's garden. He was fascinated by the way they chewed tree bark and spit out balls of a doughy substance, which they formed into a nest just the right size and shape to make a home for their young.

When he was older, Ts'ai Lun saw some farmers tear down a wasp's nest because they were afraid of being stung while they worked. He picked up the pieces of the nest. They were light in weight, but strong. He tried writing on them using the traditional Chinese brush and ink and found it was a much better writing surface than tree bark (which many people used in those days) or animal skins, which required a lot of work to prepare properly. He remembered seeing the wasps build their nests when he was a boy, and he decided to do what they did, but with an important variation. Instead of hiring many people to chew tree bark and spit it out, he mashed a huge mass of bark in a stone-lined pit, then pressed the resulting pulpy glop into long thin sheets. When dry, these became a perfect material on which people could write letters and draw wonderful brushed-ink pictures of trees, birds, cats, and tigers for which China, and later Japan, became famous.

Whether or not this tale is true, almost 2,000 years ago, China did develop a very important papermaking industry. During the next few centuries, the Chinese also made important advances in printing on paper. By 868 A.D., they were carving the characters that make up their words on blocks of wood. They inked the blocks with a paintbrush and pressed paper on them.

About 200 years later, a man named Pi Sheng invented a method of holding together clay blocks of characters to make up a complete document. Because the blocks could be separated and rearranged to print a different document, the process was called movable type. In 1313, an improvement, wooden blocks set in cases, came into use.

As a result of these inventions, it became possible for the Chinese to make books to read long before most Europeans could even write their own names. Chinese emperors were proud of their book collections. One was said to have had over 50,000 books in his personal library.

Paper Spreads Around the World. In 610 A.D., paper was introduced in Japan. Paper and, later, the techniques of papermaking were transmitted along the trade routes to the Arab world. The

10

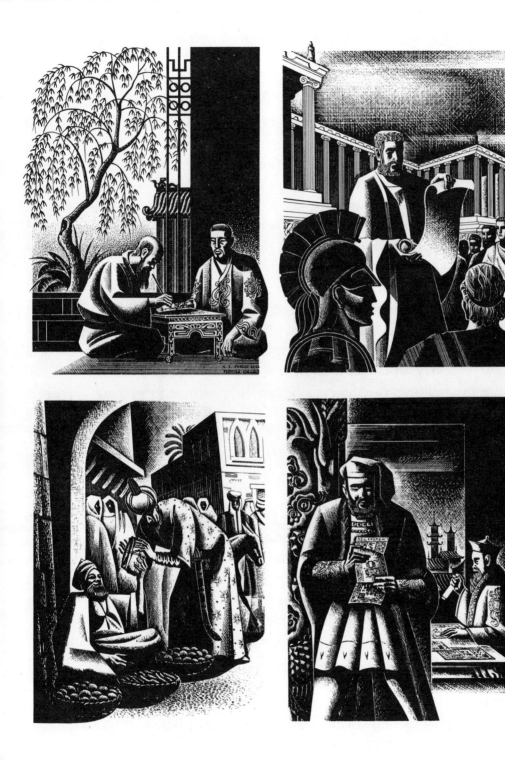

Left, the Chinese wrote on bone, bamboo, and silk before they invented paper.

Right, ancient Romans wrote their documents on parchment.

Left, by 1035 A.D., Arab merchants used paper to wrap their wares.

Right, in the 13th-century, the Chinese printed paper money.

11

Moors, who were from Morocco, brought paper to Spain around 1150. It came to Italy in 1250. (In 1266, the Italian traveler Marco Polo was amazed to find the Chinese using paper money.) Soon after, paper appeared in Germany and France, and, by 1495, in England.

A German named Johann Gutenberg is believed to be the first European to invent a printing press using movable type made of metal. By using molds filled with lead to make the type, large quantities of each letter of the alphabet were made exactly alike. The type could be rearranged at will, used repeatedly, and removed easily. The finished document had uniform lettering and could be copied again and again. Since thousands of letters are needed to write a book, this invention was revolutionary. And in 1455, Gutenberg printed a Bible on paper that he made himself.

The development of the printing press triggered an increased demand for books—and paper. Papermaking was no longer confined to the printers who made paper as they needed it, but became a major industry in its own right.

Papermaking in America began in Germantown, Pennsylvania, in 1690, when two men named William Rittenhouse and William Bradford built the first papermill, the Rittenhouse Mill. In the early 1700s, this mill was among the first recyclers in the country, using wastepaper to produce newsprint, and rags for fine paper.

Paper From Pulpwood. Although we think of trees as the main source of cellulose for papermaking, for several hundred years, linen and cotton rags provided the basic materials for the papermills of Europe and America. As the demand for paper grew, the price of these materials rose. It was clear that another method of making paper, using a more abundant material, had to be found.

In 1803, two English brothers named Henry and Sealy Fourdrinier built a papermaking machine that made the use of wood pulp practical in the production of paper. It was an improvement over a French design that had been the first to produce a continuous roll of paper, instead of one sheet at a time. The Fourdrinier machine is still used to make pulpwood paper.

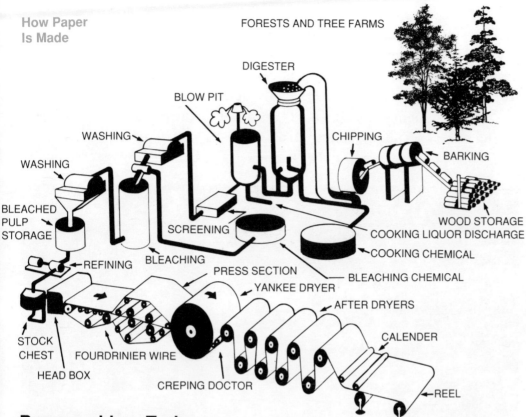

FORESTS AND TREE FARMS

DIGESTER

BLOW PIT

WASHING

WASHING

CHIPPING

BARKING

BLEACHED
PULP
STORAGE

SCREENING

WOOD STORAGE

COOKING LIQUOR DISCHARGE

COOKING CHEMICAL

REFINING

BLEACHING

PRESS SECTION

BLEACHING CHEMICAL

YANKEE DRYER

AFTER DRYERS

CALENDER

STOCK
CHEST

FOURDRINIER WIRE

HEAD BOX

CREPING DOCTOR

REEL

Paper is made from cellulose fibers—finer than human hair—that make up 50 percent of wood.

Papermaking Today

All kinds of papers are produced for all sorts of purposes. But the basic papermaking method used today, with variations to meet different needs, is much the same as it was in China 2,000 years ago—and even before that, if you consider how long the wasps have been at it. The method still requires plant fiber, most often from logs or wood chips.

There are two major techniques for turning wood into pulp. In the mechanical process, the wood is held against huge grindstones or between stone and metal serrated disks, which revolve at high speeds and thoroughly shred, beat, and separate the fibers. The pulp is mixed with water. In the chemical process, the wood is digested in a chemical solution.

Both methods produce a watery pulp that is poured over either the moving endless-belt screen of the Fourdrinier machine or a revolving screen of the cylinder machine. As the screen moves, much

13

of the water drains through the mesh. The drying pulp goes through several more finishing processes before it's shaped and completely dried into paper. The next step is called calendering: the dry paper is ironed smooth between heavy, polished rollers.

If the paper is going to be used for printing, the papermaker might apply a special coating made of clay or starch to make the surface especially smooth. Bleach may be used to turn the brownish

Paper is dried before being rolled up or cut into sheets.

pulp white, or dyes may be added to create colored paper. Rosin sizing (a substance that prevents paper from absorbing liquid) is added if the paper is to be used for water-resistant products such as wallpaper and for writing paper to keep the ink from spreading.

Giant paper cutters cut the sheets at predetermined lengths. The finished paper is either wound on huge rolls or placed flat for shipping. Then it's delivered to factories to be made into a thousand-plus useful paper products.

Recycled paper, clean and white, is ready to be used again.

Fibers for paper made from cotton or linen rags are treated very much like wood materials: they are pounded and separated into a pulp and pressed into sheets. Rag paper is high-quality paper used for important documents such as treaties, life insurance policies, deeds, and of course paper money.

Manufacturing new paper from wastepaper is similar; however, to remove contaminants, the repulping operation requires different equipment that most mills don't have. For example, printed paper has to be de-inked if it's going be used for newsprint or other new products. As the demand for recycled paper grows, more mills capable of removing contaminants are expected to be in operation.

Ancient Material, New Uses

Paper has come a long way from its limited original use in wasp-nest construction and then as a medium on which the Chinese wrote letters and drew pictures 2,000 years ago. A Japanese fable that may be a thousand years old reminds us that paper can be used for many things that Ts'ai Lun never dreamed of.

A little girl and her younger brother saw their father, a poor woodsman, arrested for accidentally chopping down a tree whose roots were partly on property that belonged to the emperor. The children begged for their father's release, but were refused. They followed the emperor everywhere, begging him to let their father go. The emperor couldn't turn around without seeing the youngsters and hearing their pleas. Finally, to get rid of them (or so he thought) he said he'd free their father if they could bring him sunlight to shine through the night's darkness, and wind to cool him in summer.

The children searched the countryside, determined to fulfill the emperor's demands. They came to the door of a hut in the darkest part of the forest. An old woman appeared. She was touched by their love for their father and said she'd give them what they were looking for.

They returned to the royal court and announced to a very surprised emperor that they had what he requested. The boy held up a paper fan and said, "Wave it and a cool wind will appear." His sister held up a paper lantern with a lit candle inside and said, "Hang it high and you will have light all night long."

The emperor freed the children's father. And before long, lanterns and paper fans were in demand all over Japan.

Although this is just a fable, it is a fact that paper is essential at home, in school, and in the workplace, and that its uses continue to grow. "Hard copies" (printed computer data) require boxes of computer paper. Facsimile machines require rolls of fax paper that eventually wind up in the trash bin. Photocopy machines use even more paper. There's even a paper towel on the market that can be used to cover food in microwave ovens. (Unlike other paper towels, it doesn't contain ingredients that can leach out and get into the food during the cooking process.)

Another fast-growing use for paper is in "drink boxes," airtight containers made of paper and lined with aluminum, plastic, or both. Other foods are packed in them as well.

More and more businesses are switching from plastic to paper packaging in response to public demand.

Drowning in the Waste Stream

True, paper is a biodegradable product. This means that it decomposes naturally and won't remain intact nearly as long as other materials like plastic. Biodegradable wastes were originally put into landfills because they were expected to break down into their organic components. As more garbage is put into these landfills, however, the oxygen needed in the breakdown process can't get through the packed mass of waste materials. The waste builds up rather than breaks down. As a result, paper may take as many as 40 years to degrade in a packed landfill, which adds to the problem of overflowing landfills across the country.

The New York City Sanitation Department has a curbside paper recycling program, as do many cities throughout the United States.

With all the paper products used today, and with the demand expected to double in a few years, paper that is thrown into the trash and isn't recycled will only add to the overflow of the solid waste stream that threatens our environment. The solid waste stream refers to the accumulation of solid waste materials that pours out of our homes, offices, and factories and winds up in a disposal facility such as a landfill or incinerator.

Since paper and paperboard (heavy paper, including cardboard and corrugated boxes) make up the largest part—more than 34 percent—of this torrent of trash, tackling the wastepaper problem is necessary to save the health of the planet.

The three most important ways to deal with the wastepaper problem are as follows:

1. *Reduce.* Reducing the country's bloated "wasteline" of paper means putting ourselves on a waste reduction diet by cutting down our demands for paper products.

● Instead of buying rolls of paper towels for household cleanup tasks, use sponges or rags the way people did for many years. Use cloth napkins and guest towels instead of paper ones.

● Instead of buying note pads for telephone messages or shopping lists, make your own using the backs of envelopes or other paper cut to size and fastened at the top with staples.

● Instead of having your groceries packed in paper bags, take canvas bags to the store and use them.

● Instead of buying expensive (and not easily recyclable) fancy wrapping paper for gifts, use more recyclable plain wrapping paper and tie it up with a bow or ribbon. Save gift wrap from presents and reuse it. Also, the comics make neat gift wrap for friends. (A little note can be put into the package explaining that you're using recyclable wrapping paper to help protect the environment.)

● Buy fewer packaged products. For example, instead of buying five pounds of potatoes in a paper sack, buy them loose.

● If you photocopy something, use both sides of the paper.

● Don't buy lined yellow pads. They are not easily recycled. Buy white pads, lined or unlined.

● When buying any paper products, choose those labeled with the symbol showing they're made of recycled paper. Less paper is added to the waste stream. Increasing sales of recycled goods encourages papermakers and manufacturers to buy wastepaper and make recycled products.

Remember: the key to reducing waste is not producing it in the first place.

2. *Reuse.* Reusing a product is another way we can reduce the solid wastes in the environment. When we reuse a paper product, we're giving it a chance to have a new life.

● Reuse envelopes and corrugated boxes for remailing.

● Rinse milk cartons, fill them with water, and then freeze them as ice packs to keep something cold or to apply to an injury.

● Reuse paper bags for Halloween or party masks. (A New York theater company called The Paper Bag Players uses paper bags as masks for different characters.) Cut out places for your eyes and nose and decorate the bag in imaginative ways.

The Paper Bag Players entertain in theaters and schools using bags and boxes for costumes and sets.

● Some paper boxes make great containers for holding pens and pencils or jewelry.

● Cereal boxes (such as Quaker Oats), which are round and come in at least two sizes, can be reused in many ways. You can store dry pasta in them. You can also use them to hold knitting yarn: place the ball of yarn in one of the boxes; punch a hole through the lid and pull the yarn out as needed.

● If you have a fireplace, tell your parents about logs made from recycled paper, which are now on sale in many supermarkets.

3. *Recycle.* Recycling is not a new process for dealing with wastepaper. Actually, used cellulose has been part of the paper-making process for centuries. Old paper and rags have often gone into the mix to produce new paper. But for a long time, most people weren't aware that recycling existed. There was no great call for recycling either. It wasn't until we faced some very serious threats to the environment that recycling became an important priority.

Environmentalists were among the first to realize the threat to our forests. The lumber industry was cutting down trees faster than new ones could grow. When trees are lost, a lot of terrible things may happen: the oxygen that is generated by the green leaves is gone; the moisture in the soil dries out; the soil erodes and, in time, turns into a desert.

The other problem was what to do with the growing mountains of wastepaper. As said before, the solid waste stream was overflowing with it.

The federal government certainly advocates recycling, but most of the efforts have been made at the local or state levels. Many of the programs are supported by the paper industry. Fortunately, paper is one of the most easily recycled products in our environment.

The American Paper Institute, an organization representing 90 percent of the paper and paperboard makers around the country, says that 26 million tons of wastepaper were collected for recycling in 1988. By 1995, the Institute expects the annual collection to reach 40 million tons. That's a lot of paper to collect and recycle, but guess what? That will still be less than half of all the available recyclable paper.

Communities around the country have started curbside collection programs where newspapers, and sometimes magazines and paperboard, are tied in bundles separated from the rest of the trash. The bundles are either picked up by the sanitation department or a waste management company working for the community. The paper is then sold to papermills for recycling into new paper products.

Some people, who used to bring their wastepaper to dumps, are now taking it to recycling centers where they receive payment based on the paper's weight. The recycling center then resells the paper to a mill.

Each ton of recycled wastepaper saves over three cubic yards of landfill space.

To Market, to Market

One of the problems with recycling is that buyers are needed for the recycled products. If there aren't enough newspapers or cardboard box manufacturers willing to use recycled paper, the market for the recyclables will be too limited to encourage more recycling.

The federal government is encouraging the use of products that contain recycled materials. At least 75 percent of state governments give preference to recycled products when purchasing supplies. Some states offer tax incentives to encourage communities to set up recycling programs. Many states are also working to encourage the construction of more de-inking plants.

Celebrities are getting into the act to help build markets for recycled paper. Singer Olivia Newton-John has told her fans that her new albums and compact discs are packaged in recycled paperboard. She's also told the employees of her 55 Koala Blue gift boutiques that they must use recycled paperboard for gift bags, boxes, and signs.

One company, Celestial Seasonings, not only uses 100 percent recycled paperboard for its herbal tea boxes, but it saves two million pounds of packaging a year because its tea bags are packed without strings, tags, staples, and individual envelopes.

Some publishers are beginning to select recycled paper for their books. The *How on Earth* books are printed on recycled paper.

Many other businesses are participating in the recycling effort, but consumers must let them know that they want to buy recycled products.

It Makes "Cents" to Recycle. Does your school band need new instruments? What about sports equipment for your Scout troop? You may be able to raise funds for many things your school or organization needs through your recycling efforts.

The American Paper Institute cites examples of young people who found out it really pays to get into recycling. For instance, the Calumet Council of the Boy Scouts of America set up a one-day drive in which 7,000 scouts from 88 communities in Chicago and northern

22

For many years, Boy Scouts and other charitable groups have been an important link in collecting old newspapers for recycling.

Indiana, working under the supervision of adults, collected nearly 500 tons of old newspapers. A local wastepaper dealer provided the collection bins and bought all the collected material. The pay-off? $8,500!

In Berwyn, Pennsylvania, the Conestoga High School Band, under the supervision of the Band Parents Association, collected over five million pounds of paper over several years. The money they earned went for new uniforms and band trips to Florida and other places.

The recycling industry provides jobs for disabled adults. One company, the Whirlpool Corporation, gave a grant to Gateway Sheltered Workshop in Berrien Springs, Michigan, to buy equipment for recycling the wastepaper from Whirlpool's offices. Disabled workers are paid to separate, sort, shred, and bale the paper before it's sold to the paper mills for recycling.

23

Making It Personal

Everyone can get involved in recycling. Here are some tips on what you can do:

● Set up a three-bin paper collection corner in your home. Put old newspapers in one; white paper (letters, envelopes) in another; and cardboard and flattened corrugated boxes in a third. (Check with your local recycling center for information on what to do with magazines. Some accept them; some do not.)

● Ask your teacher to start a paper recycling program in your classroom using the three-bin method.

● If your community doesn't have curbside pickups, you and your friends (with permission from your parents) can organize a wastepaper pickup service in your neighborhood. Since it will save them a trip to a recycling center, many of your neighbors may be happy to let you and your friends keep the entire amount paid by the dealer (especially if you plan to contribute it to a charitable cause).

● Talk to your parents about starting a recycling program where they work.

● Suggest that your parents buy recycled paper products whenever possible to help develop the market for recycled materials.

Get to Know Your Paper Facts

Once people realize that you're involved in recycling paper, they're going to expect you to know something about it. So, here are answers to some questions they may ask you:

Q: What paper is not recyclable?

A: Fax paper, carbon paper, paper that has been used to wrap food, as well as facial tissues and paper hand towels (for health reasons).

Q: Can paper be continually recycled?

A: No. Eventually, the fibers weaken and the recycled paper can no longer be broken down into the fiber strands used to produce new paper. That's why it's important to continue collecting recyclable paper for the mills.

Q: What happens if I accidentally put in paper that can't be recycled?

A: The recycling center will go through the paper before it's sent to the mills. The mills sort the batches again before the papermaking process begins. But this extra step adds to the cost of production.

Q: Why make a big deal about recycling anyway? We can always plant new trees to make wood chips, and we can burn the wastepaper, can't we?

A: Sure, we can do all that. But that doesn't help the environment. It takes years for trees to grow. As long as the paper industry is dependent on wood, forests that have so far escaped being cut are threatened. Also, burning wastepaper can increase air pollution.

Each family helps
our environment
by recycling.

Q: So what do communities do with paper that can't be recycled?

A: Some of it is burned, under carefully controlled conditions, in incinerators where the paper and other waste are the fuel for producing energy. But ash remains that must be put in landfills.

Q: What are the benefits of recycling paper?

A: Besides improving the environment now, you'll be helping to create a cleaner, healthier environment for the future. You'll have forests and wildlife to enjoy that might otherwise be destroyed by the demand for raw papermaking material.

You'll also be able to take advantage of job opportunities provided by new industries. Engineers, chemists, and designers will be needed to design more efficient recycling processes and new products from the recycled material. Waste management companies that handle wastepaper collection and delivery to papermills will expand, and new workers will be needed.

Less energy is used to produce recycled paper than pulpwood paper. As a result, less consumption of energy nationwide could mean lower fuel bills for everyone.

Q: What's wrong with putting the extra paper into landfills since it's going to decompose anyway?

A: Glad you asked that! Yes, it will decompose, someday. But most landfills are so tightly packed with trash that air doesn't circulate. It's like putting things into an airtight can. That means things that should decompose in a certain amount of time, don't.

Don't Be a Paper Tiger. A Paper Tiger is someone who pretends to be tough, but when tested, falls apart. When it comes to the environment, stand by your decision to help protect it by recycling recyclables, including paper.

Check out the fascinating projects on the following pages and, using your lively imagination, see how many things you can make by doing your own paper recycling.

2 CRAFT IT!

These recycling crafts will acquaint you with the creative things you can make from paper and boxes and the fun you can have while doing them. All of the projects are easy to do and take only a short time to make.

You can find most of the materials you need around the house, especially if you have been collecting paper and other materials for recycling. Those you don't have at home, you may need to purchase. These items are not expensive, so buy those of better quality, as they will last longer and prove more economical in the long run.

Assuming you have a pencil and scissors on hand, these will not be listed under "Materials." Other supplies you may need are paintbrushes • paints • crayons • water-based felt marking pens • glue (such as Elmer's or Sobo) • metal ruler • shellac • clear spray fixative • eraser • transparent tape • invisible mending tape • cloth-backed tapes of various colors • and a Stanley-type safety knife. When using a spray can, be sure to read its label and follow all safety precautions. Get permission from an adult before using sharp knives or razor blades.

Take care of your supplies so that they will always be ready for use. Protect your worktable with newspapers. Paintbrushes, tools, and worktables should always be cleaned after using. Paints, pastes, and other bottled materials should be kept in closed, airtight containers when not in use.

Learn to be economical. Save pieces of crayon, chalk, and paper as you will surely find a use for them.

Store your supplies and collection of recyclables in a box, cabinet, or closet. You will soon have a "treasure chest" from which you can create many new and wonderful things.

PAPER RECYCLING IDEAS

DISCARDS	SOURCES & NOTES	SUGGESTED REUSES
Boxes	Gift, mailing, food packages, shoe boxes, shirt box, etc.	Recover & decorate for gifts, dioramas, doll furniture, games, peep boxes, bird feeders, pencil holders, castles, houses, & towns
Calendars	Outdated	Pictures for decoupage, greeting cards; numbers for flash cards, toy clock, games, dollhouse numbers
Christmas & other greeting cards		Decoupage, make new cards, gift tags, paper mosaics, ornaments & tree trims, pictures for scenes
Corrugated cartons	Large shipping boxes	Storage, playhouse or castle, stage props, masks, constructions, dollhouse, puppet stage
	Cut sides for flat items	Backing for pictures, posters, mailing flat items
Crepe paper		Baskets, costumes, flowers, weaving
Drinking cups	Wash out	Doll furniture, string holder, seedling planter, constructions
Egg cartons	Clean	Store small items, collections, start seeds, toys, decorations, flowers
Envelopes & linings		Collage, decorations, pictures, file recipes or notes
Gift-wrapping paper	Remove tapes, press flat	Reuse for wrapping smaller gifts, dollhouse wallpaper, book covers, covering boxes & tubes, collage
Junk mail	Use unprinted sections, return envelopes	Notes, lists, drawings; relabel & reuse return envelopes; store coupons, pictures in sturdy envelopes
Laundry or cereal box cardboard		Stiffeners for mailings, art or collage background, constructions, sewing cards, templates, patterns
Magazines & glossy catalogs	Use colorful pages	Paper beads, gift cards, puzzle pictures, scrapbook, homework projects

DISCARDS	SOURCES & NOTES	SUGGESTED REUSES
Milk cartons	Rinse well, as soon as emptied	Boats, bird feeders, seedling planters, houses & towns, storage, papier-mâché vases
Newspapers		Papier-mâché, protect surfaces, pet training, hats, collages, packing material
Paper bags		Scrapbook pages, masks, puppets, hats, wrapping small packages, book covers
Paper, colored or printed		Confetti, scrapbook pages, decoupage, cornucopias, constructions
Paper napkins	Use clean parts	Papier-mâché, paper doll clothes, decoupage designs
Paper plates	Wipe well with damp cloth	Note holder, masks, constructions, round frames for pictures
Stamps	Canceled	Collection, decoupage, box decorations, pictures in dollhouse
Telephone books, newsprint catalogs		Pressing flowers & leaves, papier-mâché, scrapbook pages
Tissue paper		Transparencies, papier-mâché, comb kazoo, flowers, die transfer art
Tubes, mailing & other: centers of gift wrap, paper towels, bathroom tissue		Turret on cardboard box castles, puppets, pen holders, totem pole, doll cradle, bracelet, center core for making papier-mâché animals
Wallpaper	Leftovers, samples	Cover boxes, shelves, drawers, gifts; paper beads, book covers, bookmarks, dollhouse wallpaper
Wax paper		Protect surface when using glue
Wrapping paper (brown)		Stage costumes, large murals, wrapping for shipping, shelf & drawer liners

SIMPLE PAPER WHISTLE

A simple fold, a basic cut, and you have a whistle. All you need is a piece of note or typewriter paper and a pair of scissors.

INSTRUCTIONS

1. Trace outline of whistle on paper as in diagram. Cut out along edges.
2. Fold in half.
3. Fold back the two ends.
4. Cut a small diamond shape in the center.

How to use: Hold the whistle by the ends. Open slightly and blow. Have fun whistling a happy tune!

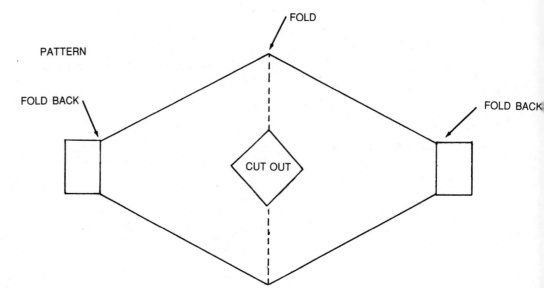

FOLD

PATTERN

FOLD BACK

FOLD BACK

CUT OUT

PAPER FINGER-TRAP

Want to play a trick on a friend? Make this trap, and ask him or her to try to get out of this tight squeeze.

INSTRUCTIONS

1. On a 6" x 12" piece of heavy wrapping paper, draw two parallel lines, 8" long and 2" apart. Cut slits along parallel lines.

2. Roll paper into a tube with a diameter of about 1/2". Start rolling the cut edge (see diagram) first, so that when the tube is completed this edge will be on the inside.

3. Glue the outside edge firmly to the outside of the tube. Let glue dry.

How to use: When the forefingers are placed into the open ends of the tube, they cannot be pulled out easily. The harder the fingers are pulled, the tighter the trap holds. To release the fingers, push fingers toward center of tube, and pull one finger out at a time.

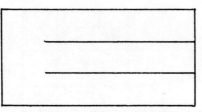

HEAVY WRAPPING PAPER

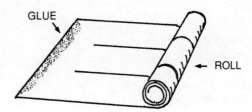

GLUE

ROLL

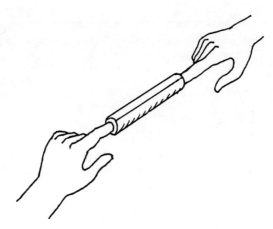

BASIC PAPER HOUSE

This simple project serves as an example of how easy it is to work with paper. Just reach out for some stiff paper and a few materials to begin to learn the art of folding.

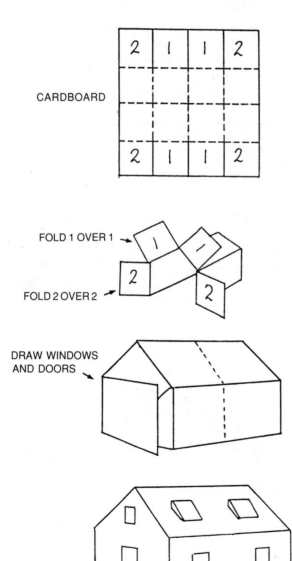

CARDBOARD

FOLD 1 OVER 1

FOLD 2 OVER 2

DRAW WINDOWS AND DOORS

MATERIALS
- Stiff paper or cardboard
- Scissors or Stanley-type safety knife
- Glue
- Paint and paintbrush, or crayons
- Ruler

INSTRUCTIONS
1. Cut out an 8" square.
2. Mark off all edges every 2". Use ruler to draw heavy lines and dotted lines as in diagram. Mark with numbers as you see them.
3. Cut all heavy lines. Fold on all dotted lines.
4. Fold 1 over 1 and 2 over 2, on each end.
5. Decide where windows and doors should go. Unfold paper, and draw them in. Color with paints or crayons.
6. Refold the house and glue front and back flaps in place.

JAPANESE LANTERNS

The Japanese and other Oriental people add charm and special atmosphere to their environment with beautiful paper lanterns. From sturdy and stiff shiny papers, you can design attractive lamps.

MATERIALS

- Metallic wrapping paper or other heavy paper
- Scissors or Stanley-type safety knife
- Ruler
- Glue or clear mending tape
- Paint and paintbrushes, crayons or stickers (optional)

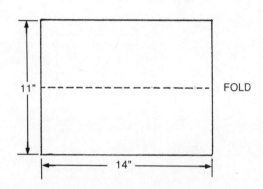

INSTRUCTIONS

1. Cut out a piece of metallic wrapping paper, 11" x 14". Fold it in half.

2. Keep folded edge on the bottom. Beginning 1/2" from the top, draw lines 1/2" apart. Starting from the bottom, carefully cut slits.

3. Open paper and overlap the two edges. Fasten together with glue or clear tape.

4. Cut out a small strip of metallic paper for a handle and glue or tape it to inside of lantern.

5. If you wish, decorate top and bottom of your lantern with paint or small stickers.

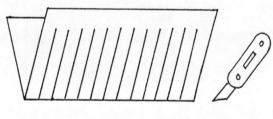

CUT SLITS 1/2" APART

VARIATIONS

Try different sizes of paper. Cut strips diagonally. Use a French curve for an interesting effect.

OPEN AND GLUE

33

POP-UP GREETING CARDS

You can create amazing pop-ups like the ones you see in books, magazines, and greeting cards. Here's one form of pop-up you can make to send to someone special.

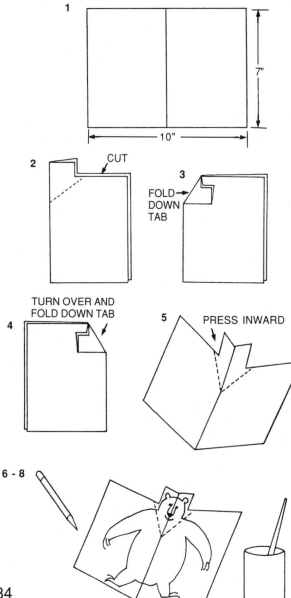

MATERIALS

- Paper of various colors and weight
- Crayons or felt markers
- Paste or glue
- Pen

INSTRUCTIONS

1. With scissors, cut a piece of paper, 7" x 10". Fold in half.

2. Cut out a section along the upper edge, as shown.

3. Fold down tab on an angle.

4. Turn paper over and fold tab down against side.

5. Open paper showing diagonal creases with tab at top. Fold back again along the original centerfold, pressing diagonal creases and tab inward.

6. Draw a humorous face or figure (or paste one in) on the pop-up. Add artwork to complete design. Neatly write your message in ink.

7. When the card is opened, the picture you drew will pop up.

8. Finish card by making a design on the cover.

VARIATIONS

There are many ways to create amusing pop-ups. Practice with paper of different sizes and shapes, and try cutting out other sections.

34

MILK CARTON ORGANIZER

This handy organizer will be useful on a desk, in the kitchen or bathroom, or anywhere in your home.

MATERIALS

- Four 1 quart or 1/2 gallon milk cartons
- Scissors or Stanley-type safety knife or safety-edge razor blade
- Glue or paste
- Metal ruler
- Pencil
- Paint and paintbrushes
- Materials for decoration, such as colored tape and stickers

INSTRUCTIONS

1. Rinse the milk cartons. Dry thoroughly.

2. Lay the first one on your workspace. With your pencil and ruler, draw lines as shown, and cut away tops. Repeat for each carton.

3. Paint or decorate with colored tape, stickers, or anything else you can think of.

   Use the cartons separately or glued together.

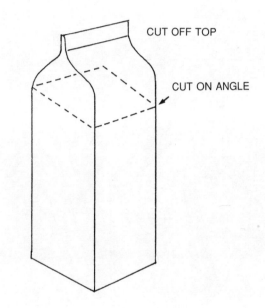

CUT OFF TOP

CUT ON ANGLE

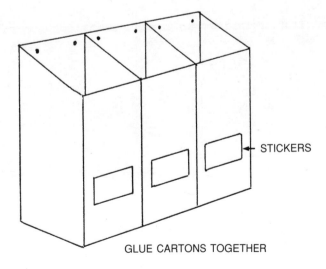

STICKERS

GLUE CARTONS TOGETHER

35

SIX-PACK TOOL BOX

This useful item, recycled from an old six-pack carrier, can be a carrying case, tool box, or desktop supply holder. Use your imagination and see what other ideas occur to you.

MATERIALS

- Six-pack carrying carton
- Crayons
- Paint and paintbrushes
- Alphabet stickers or stencils, or tape (all optional)

INSTRUCTIONS

1. Clean the carton thoroughly.

2. Paint and decorate the carton as you choose. Let dry.

3. You can letter a name or any other label with paint, stencils, stickers, or colored tape.

VARIATIONS

For a desktop supply holder, you can keep pencils in one section, scissors and rulers in another. Cut out divider between two sections to fit in envelopes or other large items.

PAPER-BAG MASKS

Here's a fun project for parties, family get-togethers, or holiday events at school. Like the The Paper Bag Players theater company, make up your own plays using the characters you've created with your paper-bag masks.

MATERIALS

- Large paper bags
- Paint and paintbrushes, felt markers, or crayons
- Glue or paste
- Needle and thread (optional)
- Items for trim, such as beads, earrings, feathers, yarn, cotton, ribbon, flowers, etc.

INSTRUCTIONS

1. Place a bag over your head. With pencil, carefully make marks on the outside of the bag where your eyes, nose, mouth, and ears are.

2. Remove bag and draw face using pencil marks as guidelines.

3. Cut out openings for eyes and mouth. You may cut nose and ear openings, too.

4. Paint or crayon on lips, eyelashes, and cheeks.

5. You can paint or draw on eyebrows, hair, and a mustache. Or glue on cotton, yarn, or colored paper.

6. For a beard, slash strips in the bottom of the bag, or glue on cotton or yarn.

7. Glue or sew beads or earrings to the ears. Add feathers, flowers, or bows to the hair. What else can you think of?

VARIATIONS

Paper bags can be turned into crowns or hats—add feathers, flowers, and other trim. Using extra-large shopping bags (handles removed), design quick costumes to match your masks for an on-the-spot theatrical performance.

DECORATED STORAGE BOXES

Do you have trouble keeping your room or closet in order? Here's an easy way to get organized—make matching boxes to store sweaters, gloves, and odds-and-ends. These decorated storage boxes make great gifts, too.

MATERIALS

- Suit box and cover, hat box and cover, and/or any boxes large enough for your storing needs
- Wallpaper or gift wrap (or you can hand-decorate plain paper)
- Glue or paste
- Ruler

INSTRUCTIONS

For Suit Box:

1. Lay the cover of the box on paper. Using pencil and ruler, carefully measure around it, allowing extra paper to cover sides and a little extra for folding over the inside edges.

2. Cut out a small square from each corner of the paper.

3. Spread glue on the back of the paper and neatly place it over the cover. Smooth it down so that there are no air bubbles, and take care not to get glue on the outside.

4. Wait for cover to dry before placing it on box.

For Hat Box:

1. Measure and then cut paper (may choose pattern to match suit box) so that it is large enough to cover the entire box.

2. Lay cover on paper, and cut a circle about 4" larger in diameter. Along the edge, cutting about 4" into the circle, cut out small triangles so that you will get a neat fit when gluing it to cover.

3. Now assemble. Glue sides on box and circle on cover. Let dry before using.

1.

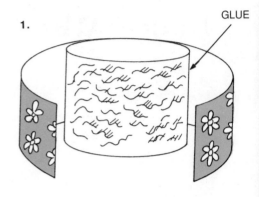

GLUE

2.

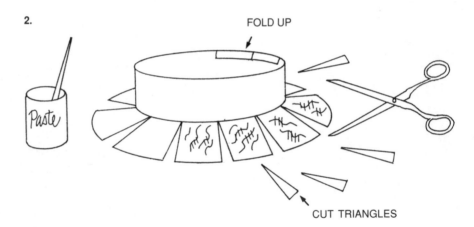

FOLD UP

CUT TRIANGLES

3.

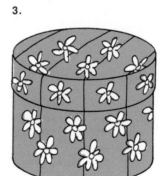

PORTABLE TELEVISION SET

Turn off the family television set and announce that you will appear on television at a scheduled time. Then make your own portable TV and offer a production.

MATERIALS

- Large corrugated box
- Stanley-type safety knife
- Metal ruler
- Glue
- Metal paper fasteners
- Quick-drying latex wall paint (tempera paints will do, but you'll need a lot)
- Wide paintbrushes
- Clear plastic wrap (Saran Wrap)
- Colored tape (optional)

INSTRUCTIONS

1. Neatly cut off all the flaps of the open end of your box. (For best results, with safety knife, cut carefully against metal ruler.) This open end should fit over your head.

2. Draw a large rectangle for your TV screen. Leave enough room all around for a frame, with an extra-wide border at the bottom as this is where you will place the dials. Carefully cut out rectangle.

3. On one of the discarded flaps, draw three or four circles for your dials. Cut them out. Attach on bottom border with fasteners.

4. Cut out a piece of clear plastic wrap large enough to fit and cover the inside of the frame. Tape or glue it tightly in place. This is your television screen.

5. Cut a strip of leftover corrugated cardboard about 9" x 1 1/2" for a carrying handle. Attach handle to the top of the TV set with two fasteners.

6. Paint your set with available colors. Paint dials black or other color. Add tape stripes, stickers, or other decorations for visual interest.

7. Slip the portable television cabinet over your head and make believe you're on TV.

   You're now ready to be a "talking head": give a speech, tell jokes, sing songs—entertain!

VARIATION

For a TV Puppet Theater, cut a large window from a very large box. Place it on a covered bridge table (see diagram). Cut out the back of the box. Sew or pin a piece of dark material over a curtain rod. Extend the rod through the sides of the box—not more than 2" from the top and back. Seated on a chair behind the curtain, you can manipulate and move your hand puppets freely. You (and a partner) can create theater productions that feature singing, jokes, funny voices, and a variety of characters.

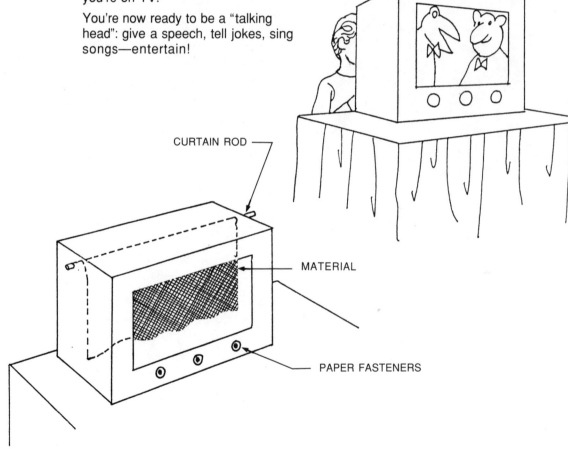

CURTAIN ROD

MATERIAL

PAPER FASTENERS

THREE-D PICTURE FRAME ART

You and your family may receive gifts or appliances that come in useful boxes. These can be used in many projects at school or home. And they're great for gift giving—which is recycling at its best.

MATERIALS

- Box cover about 2" deep
- Paint and paintbrushes
- Glue
- Cardboard
- Cork
- Magazines for cutting out pictures (optional)

INSTRUCTIONS

1. Paint or decorate box cover on both sides. Solid colors work best.
2. For a background on the inside back wall, paint a scene or cut a scenic picture from a magazine. Glue it down neatly.

3. Paint people, animals, and/or other objects on scrap pieces of cardboard. Or cut out and mount small pictures with glue. Cut around pictures to trim off excess cardboard. Glue figures to small slices of cork to make them stand.

4. Move them around on floor of picture. Space them in different depths for a full three-dimensional effect. When you are satisfied with their position, glue them to the floor.

VARIATIONS

It can be fun to use photos of your family (with permission) and set them against unusual backgrounds. Try gluing different shapes around frame for unique decorations.

CUT OUT PHOTO

DRAW OR CUT OUT PICTURE

44

FOLD-AWAY HOUSE

Solve your housing problem! Here's an instant house (or apartment) for tiny dolls, 4" high or smaller. If the doll family expands, so can the house. You simply add more cardboard panels for all the extra rooms needed. And it's very easy to store away.

MATERIALS

- Three pieces of cardboard, each about 16" x 8 1/2" (from boxes, shirts, or corrugated cartons)
- Invisible mending tape
- Magazines for cutting out pictures
- Drawing paper
- Paint, crayons, or water-based felt markers
- Glue
- Ruler
- Stanley-type safety knife

INSTRUCTIONS

1. Score and fold each cardboard in half crosswise.
2. Tape the three folded cardboards together, leaving a small space between the edges to make a flexible joint. The three folds should be facing in the same direction to get the "accordion" effect.
3. Cut out a house front from a magazine and paste in on the first panel (or draw and paint it on). Using safety knife, cut two sides of the door frame so that it can open and close. The doorway should be high enough for your dolls to be able to walk through without bumping their heads!

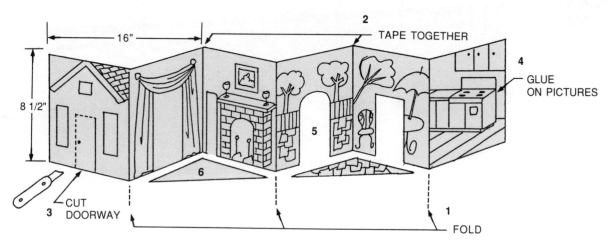

4. Plan the order you want the rooms in, using both sides of the cardboard. Draw or glue magazine cutout scenes appropriate to each room: furniture, kitchen equipment, windows, and so on. Leave space for doors. If you want to have a patio or garden, choose one pair of panels (perhaps, 4 and 5, as in diagram) on which to draw or glue an outdoor scene.

5. Cut out doorways (as in 3) or open arches in the other walls so that the dolls can go from room to room.

6. You can also add flooring. On triangular pieces of drawing paper to fit the space, draw a rug, tiles for the kitchen, and flagstones for the patio.

VARIATIONS

Make small furniture to fit in the rooms. To build a two-story house, lay a shirt cardboard on top of the open panels and place another set of rooms on top of that.

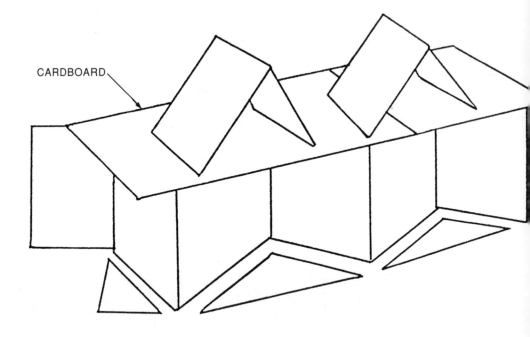

CARDBOARD

CORRUGATED CARTON DOLLHOUSE

Boxes and dollhouses go well together. From simple to elegant—how elaborate you want to make your house is up to you. A corrugated carton that is about 18" x 12" x 10"—the kind in which canned goods are packed—is a good size. (If you don't have one at home, ask your grocer for a clean one.)

MATERIALS

- Corrugated cardboard carton
- Metal ruler
- Glue
- Stanley-type safety knife
- Cardboard
- Plastic tape
- Metal paper fastener (for door knob)
- Latex house paint
- Wallpaper
- Clear spray protective coating
- Colored paper, felt, fabric, or rug remnant

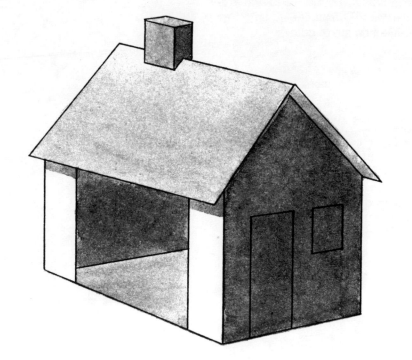

INSTRUCTIONS

1. If inside flaps on the bottom of carton are not sealed, glue them closed. If they do not meet, cut a piece of cardboard with safety knife and glue it over the space. This will be the floor of the house.

2. Cut out a wide opening from long side of carton.

3. Mark off window openings with pencil. With the safety knife against the metal ruler, cut out door and windows.

4. To make a peaked roof, make a mark in the center of top edge of each short flap. On each, draw lines from the mark to the bottom corners of the flap. Cut along the lines, with the knife against the metal ruler.

5. Bend the long flaps up to meet the peaks and fasten together with tape.

6. Cut a long piece of cardboard for the roof, 1" larger on all sides than the roof frame. Score and fold the roof cardboard down center, lengthwise. Glue it on top of house.

7. To make chimney, measure, cut, and fold a strip of cardboard, following the dimensions in the diagram.

8. Bend at the folds and glue or tape the chimney together.

9. Place chimney on roof. With pencil, draw an outline around chimney to get the right size needed for chimney opening. Carefully cut out a chimney opening on roof. Put chimney into opening and fasten in place with mending tape.

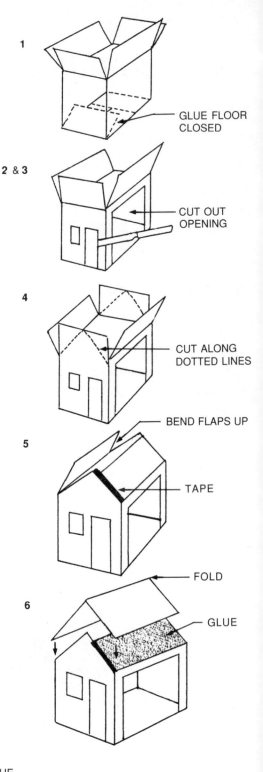

1 — GLUE FLOOR CLOSED

2 & 3 — CUT OUT OPENING

4 — CUT ALONG DOTTED LINES

BEND FLAPS UP

5 — TAPE

FOLD

6 — GLUE

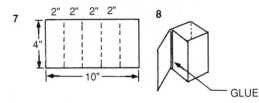

7   2" 2" 2" 2"   8

4"

10"

GLUE

48

10. Tape all cut edges of house to give it a smooth, finished look.

11. Paint outside of the house and let dry thoroughly.

12. Spray outside of house with clear spray protective finish.

13. Glue wallpaper to inside walls of house and colored paper, fabric, or rug remnant to the floor for carpeting.

VARIATION

Two, three, and four similar boxes can be set on top of and next to one another to enlarge your house.

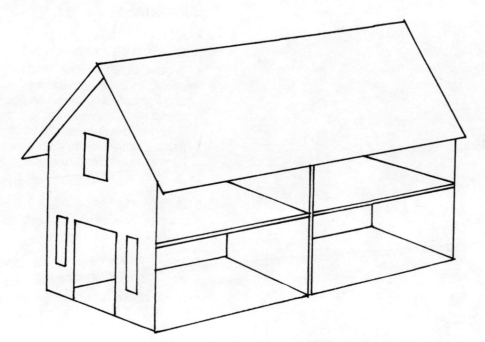

DOLLHOUSE FURNITURE

No dollhouse is complete without furniture. Your choices are limit-less. You be the decorator and designer and create old-fashioned or very modern furnishings and accessories for each room. Living room, bedroom, and other household furniture can be made as ornate as you like by adding colorful paper or fabric scraps, sponges, clay, clear or colored soap, and all kinds of plastics. Here we'll focus on suggestions for fashioning furniture out of paper, cardboard, and corrugated boxes.

MATERIALS

- All types of heavy paper, cardboard, and corrugated paperboard
- Scraps saved in your "treasure chest," such as matchboxes, soap and toothbrush boxes, can lids, small round plastic containers, fabrics, sponges, small pieces of wood, mag-azine pictures, cotton, toothpicks, pipe cleaners, and thread spools
- Glue
- Spray paint
- Stanley-type safety knife
- Metal ruler
- Colored tapes
- Water-based felt markers
- Metal paper fasteners

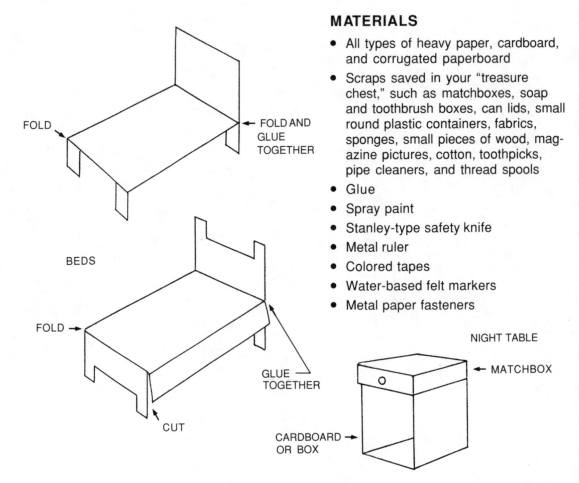

FOLD

FOLD AND GLUE TOGETHER

BEDS

FOLD

GLUE TOGETHER

CUT

NIGHT TABLE

MATCHBOX

CARDBOARD OR BOX

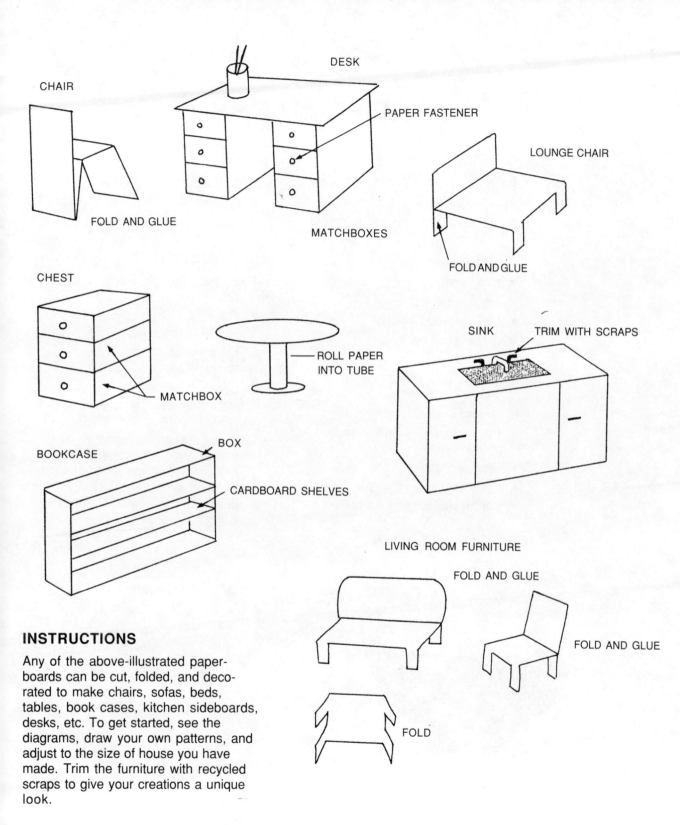

CHAIR

FOLD AND GLUE

DESK

PAPER FASTENER

MATCHBOXES

LOUNGE CHAIR

FOLD AND GLUE

CHEST

MATCHBOX

ROLL PAPER
INTO TUBE

SINK

TRIM WITH SCRAPS

BOOKCASE

BOX

CARDBOARD SHELVES

LIVING ROOM FURNITURE

FOLD AND GLUE

FOLD AND GLUE

FOLD

INSTRUCTIONS

Any of the above-illustrated paper-boards can be cut, folded, and decorated to make chairs, sofas, beds, tables, book cases, kitchen sideboards, desks, etc. To get started, see the diagrams, draw your own patterns, and adjust to the size of house you have made. Trim the furniture with recycled scraps to give your creations a unique look.

PAPIER-MÂCHÉ BOWL

Papier-mâché crafts are a fascinating way to recycle. Using old newspapers, you can create an attractive bowl. This works well for trays and other objects, too.

MATERIALS

- 1 cup flour
- 4 cups cold water
- Oil of cloves (optional)
- Large pot
- Storage jar
- Bowl or other object to be used for a mold
- Newspaper
- Paint (such as tempera) and paintbrushes
- Fine sandpaper
- Petroleum jelly (Vaseline)
- Cardboard, larger than bowl
- Shellac

INSTRUCTIONS

1. Protect workspace with newspapers.
2. Put flour in pot and gradually add water. Blend well.
3. Let stand about 20 minutes, until flour is dissolved.
4. Cook mixture over low heat. Stir constantly so mixture doesn't stick to pot or burn.
5. When mixture becomes transparent, remove from heat and cool slightly. Stir before pouring into jar. Keep covered until ready to use. (You may keep paste in refrigerator

ADD WATER

ST

COOK AT LOW HEAT

for several days. If you add a few drops of oil of cloves, it keeps longer.)

6. Cut strips of newspaper in various widths.

7. Lay bowl—top down—on cardboard. Smear a thin, even coat of Vaseline all over the bowl and on the cardboard surrounding it.

8. Dip strips of newspaper into paste (if paste is stored in a jar, pour it into a bowl or pot for easier dipping). Coat them well.

9. Crisscross strips in layers over the bowl to desired thickness, smoothing each one down so that there are no seams or air bubbles. Let dry thoroughly.

10. Sandpaper surface of bowl so it is nice and smooth.

11. Cut around rim of bowl and remove original bowl.

12. Paint papier-mâché bowl inside and out with your favorite designs.

13. When dry, coat with shellac.

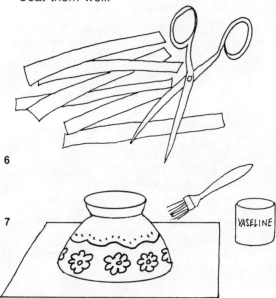

6

7

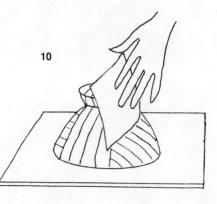

10

11

REMOVE BOWL

8

9

12. & 13.

VARIATIONS

There are many other papier-mâché techniques and unlimited projects that you can create. Check out your library for information.

BASIC PAPER KITE

Everyone should make a kite at least once to discover the joy of seeing your own creation soar into the air and reach heights limited only by the length of your string and the wind conditions. It is not difficult to do with paper and a few other materials.

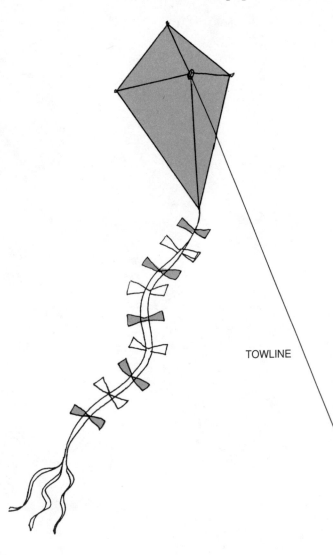

TOWLINE

MATERIALS

- Two pieces of large, wide wrapping paper (almost any kind of light paper will do)
- Two 1/4" square light wood sticks in 1 yd lengths
- Ball of fishline or kite string (regular string will do, but is not as strong)
- Stanley-type safety knife
- Glue
- Metal or plastic ring (from drapery or shower curtain)
- Light polyester, rayon, or nylon rags (such as worn-out shirts)
- Paper for bows
- Ruler or yardstick

INSTRUCTIONS

1. Using safety knife, cut wood lengths as in diagram. For spine of kite, measure 30" and cut. For crosspiece, measure 25" and cut.

2. Cut small notch of same size in each end of the sticks.

3. Measure 7 1/2" down the spine and mark off. Measure 1/4" from that mark and make another mark.

4. Now measure 12 1/2" to the exact center of the crosspiece and make a mark. (To make sure you have the center, try to balance stick on your finger at the mark. If it balances, you have exact center.)

5. Position crosspiece between the two marks on the spine. Check that exact center of the crosspiece is on exact center of the two marks.

6. Tie sticks together by crisscrossing string around both sticks where they are crossed. Knot securely. Apply glue around string and knot.

7. Put this frame over a large piece of wrapping paper. Draw a line around the frame (as shown) adding at least a 3/4" margin on all sides.

8. Cut paper along penciled guideline.

9. Glue frame to the paper. Let dry.

10. Cut a piece of string the length of the spine plus 6" extra. Tie the end around top of spine securing it through notch. Pull other end through small metal or plastic ring, attaching it in the same way to bottom of spine.

11. Similarly, tie another piece of string (about 5" longer than the crosspiece) to one end of crosspiece, pulling it through ring and tying it to other end. You now have a bridle for your kite.

12. Make sure all four ends are tied securely, and trim off excess string.

13. For a towline, tie end of a full ball of string, or a very, very long piece, to the ring.

14. Add a 10' tail of rags to the end of the spine. (A very long polyester scarf will do.)

15. Tie paper bows to tail 1' apart. Add a colorful light rag streamer to end of tail.

16. Wind towline onto a stick that will easily rotate in your hands, so that you can release and retract string as needed. Now you are ready to "go fly a kite."

VARIATIONS

Based on this simple model, there is no limit to the kinds of kites you can design and experiment with. The subject of kites is fascinating, and you can get books from the library to find out more about them.

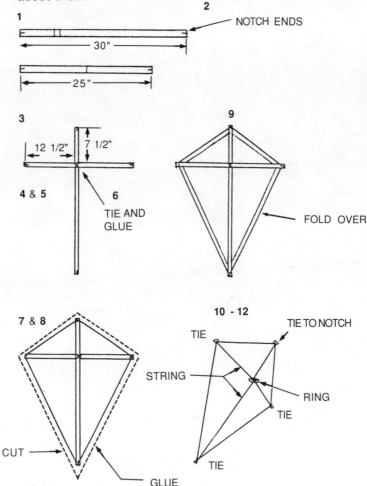

55

PAPER BEAD JEWELRY

Making jewelry from paper has a long and honorable tradition. Use colored paper from holiday gift wrapping, metallic papers, and bright-colored magazine pages to create jewelry for yourself and for gift giving. (These materials are perfect for craft projects because they are not usually suitable for public recycling programs; so save them to make beautiful creations.)

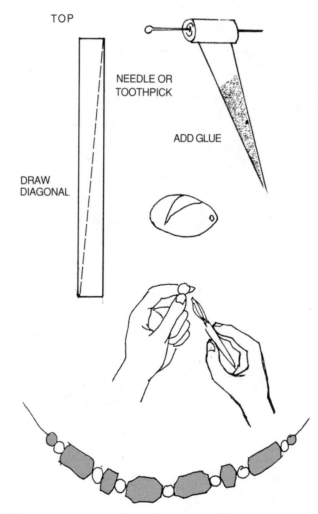

TOP

NEEDLE OR TOOTHPICK

ADD GLUE

DRAW DIAGONAL

MATERIALS

- Tracing paper
- Cardboard
- Magazines or gift wrapping
- Glue
- Toothpicks, or knitting needle or skewer
- Fishing line or dental floss
- Beads (from a necklace, broken or no longer used)
- Spray on finish or medium gloss from art supply store (optional)

INSTRUCTIONS

1. To make a bead pattern, draw a rectangle on cardboard. (A good size to begin with is 1" x 11".) Draw a diagonal line from one corner to another, as shown. Cut out one triangle. Top will be width of bead. Try various triangle sizes until you get bead desired.

2. Trace the triangle on colored magazine picture or wrapping paper.

3. Starting at wide end, roll triangle over toothpick. Place glue on lower half of the triangle. Carefully

continue rolling to tip. Slip bead off toothpick. Repeat, making enough beads for a necklace.

4. To make durable, if desired, spray with clear finish. (If making just a few beads, clear nail polish will do.)

5. Decide on length of necklace. It should be long enough to fit over your head. Cut a piece of fishing line several inches longer than desired necklace length.

6. String on beads, alternating beads from old necklace with the paper beads. When long enough, tie ends together and push tips back into last beads to hide ends. (If you use string that is not as stiff as fishing line, you may need to use a sewing needle with a large eye to string beads.)

VARIATIONS

If you'd like a necklace with three dangling beads, string the necklace to its center, alternating the paper beads with small round beads and ending with a small bead. Going around small bead, turn string up through adjoining paper bead. Add another small bead, a paper bead, and small bead. Again, turn string up through paper bead and add round bead. Repeat for third dangle. Continue alternating beads to string rest of necklace. Tie as in step 6, making sure that the dangles are centered.

TURN STRING
UP THROUGH BEAD

DANGLES

GLOSSARY

Biodegradable. Capable of being broken down into its basic components through the action of bacteria and oxygen. Everything that was once alive is biodegradable. (The prefix "bio" means life.) Paper, for example, is biodegradable since it is made from cellulose fibers, which were once part of a living tree or other plant.

Calendering. The process in which newly made paper is ironed between heavy rollers to produce a smooth finish.

Cellulose. The chief part of the cell walls of plants, sometimes referred to as vegetable or plant fiber. It is the major ingredient in papermaking. The most common source of cellulose used for papermaking is wood. Others are cotton and linen rags.

Contaminant. Undesirable material that causes problems in recycling.

De-inking. A process for removing ink from recycled wastepaper before it's repulped.

Fiber. In papermaking, fiber refers to the parts of a plant made of cellulose, the material that is turned into pulp and then into paper.

Movable type. Separate blocks of type, each engraved with a letter. The type pieces are set to form a document, put into a frame, and placed in a printing press. After being inked, paper is pressed down on the type to pick up the inked impression. This process is called printing.

Paper mill. Where paper is produced from raw materials.

Papyrus. A reed plant grown in Egypt. It was the first plant used to manufacture writing materials. The similar Greek word *papyros* is the root of our word paper. But unlike true paper, it is pressed and so retains much of its original structure of natural interconnected fibers, whereas paper is, literally, beaten to a pulp.

Parchment. A writing material made from the skin of sheep and goats. It's one of the oldest writing materials and is still used for some important documents and scrolls.

Printing. A method of transferring letters from inked type to paper or other material. The Chinese invented the first printing method in 868 A.D. using wooden blocks. In the 11th century, they also invented the first movable type using separate clay pieces for the Chinese characters and, in the 14th century, using wood. Later the Koreans invented metal type. But a German goldsmith, Johann Gutenberg, is credited with using the first movable metal type in Europe and developing the printing press. About 1455, he produced the Bible for the first time on a printing press. It later became known as the Gutenberg Bible. A few rare copies exist in museums and libraries.

Pulp. The mass that remains after plant materials, such as wood, wood chips, or linen or cotton rags, have been reduced to cellulose fibers and mixed with water to form a dough-like material that is then processed into paper. The two most common methods of manufacturing pulp from wood are mechanical and chemical. In the mechanical method, machines separate the fibers from the wood to make groundwood pulp. In the chemical method, pulp becomes almost pure cellulose, prepared from wood chips boiled under pressure with chemicals. Chemical pulp is brighter and stronger than groundwood pulp.

Rag paper. A high-quality paper used for paper currency and other important documents. It is made from the cellulose fibers in pieces of cotton or linen rags that are boiled with lime to remove grease and colored dyes, and then placed in a vat and reduced to single strands of pulpy fiber by sharp knives that are mounted on a revolving drum. The pulp is then pressed into sheets. Heavy weights squeeze out much of the water. The newly made paper is left to air dry before going through several other finishing processes.

Recyclable. The ability of a material to be reprocessed for reuse; anything made of such material (commonly glass, aluminum, paper, tin, plastic, iron, steel, and oil).

Recycle. To turn waste products into new ones. With paper, the waste materials are repulped, and processed into new paper products.

Reduce. To cut down on waste by cutting down on the demand for products that can add to the solid waste stream.

Repulping. Recycling wastepaper into pulp for papermaking.

Reuse. To use again or to find new uses for a product.

Sizing. Fillers added to porous materials. In papermaking, a substance called rosin is added to paper used for printing to keep ink from spreading or to make it water resistant.

Solid waste stream. The movement of all garbage and trash, including household discards and industrial materials, from their source to landfills, incinerators, and recycling centers.

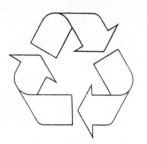

FIND OUT MORE

In theory almost everything can be recycled, but in practice a lot depends on you and your community. Listed here are the most common items that can be recovered and recycled before they go into the solid waste stream:

Paper. Newspaper, books, magazines, office papers, commercial print, corrugated packaging, folding cartons, cardboard, bags

Glass. Beer/soda bottles, wine/spirits bottles, food containers

Metal. Ferrous metal (iron and steel), including food and beverage cans, appliances, automobiles, aluminum, including soda cans, lead (car batteries), other non-ferrous (such as copper and brass)

Plastic. Plates and cups, clothing and shoes, soft drink bottles, milk bottles, containers, bags, wraps

Rubber. Tires, clothing and shoes

Textiles and *Leather.* Clothing and shoes

Other Organic Material. Food, yard wastes, wood chips

Motor Oil.

Items not easily recyclable are oily rags, household batteries, paper mixed with food, disposable diapers, and other multi-material products that can't readily be separated into reusable materials.

A material is truly recyclable only if there is a recycling system in place. Successful recycling depends upon having the necessary technology to collect, sort, and process recoverable materials, as well as finding a market for them. Your community may be capable of providing programs for only a few of these items. To find recyclers outside your community, look in the yellow pages of a telephone directory under such headings as Recycling Centers, Waste Reduction, Waste Paper, Scrap Metal, etc. for businesses devoted to salvaging waste. However, it may not be economically wise to spend a lot of time and gasoline to find a far-off recycler. Your best bet is to promote and expand existing programs in your community.

We would like to acknowledge the following organizations for their help. They can provide you, too, with information to increase your knowledge and help you in your recycling efforts.

Companies and Organizations

American Paper Institute
260 Madison Ave.
New York, NY 10016
(212) 340-0626
Booklet: *Paper and Paper Manufacturing.*

Fort Howard Corp.
P.O. Box 19130
Green Bay, WI 54307

Franklin Associates
4121 W. 83rd St.
Prairie Village, KS 66208
(913) 649-2225
They are environmental consultants for the EPA and other organizations.

Georgia Pacific, Corp.
133 Peachtree St.
Atlanta, GA 30303

National Solid Waste Management Association
1730 Rhode Island Ave., NW, Ste. 1000
Washington, DC 20036
(202) 659-4613

Pennsylvania Department of Environmental Resources
Bureau of Waste Management
P.O. Box 2063
Harrisburg, PA 17105-2063
(717) 787-7382
Or write your own state environmental agency for information.

Pima Magazine
Paper Industry Management Association
2400 E. Oakton St.
Arlington Heights, IL 60005

Scott Paper Co.
2400 Lakeshore Dr.
Muskegon, MI 49443
Booklet: *It's a Paper World.*

Solar Box Cookers International
1724 11th St.
Sacramento, CA 95814
(916) 444-6616
They will send you information on how to build a solar stove using corrugated cardboard, newspaper, and other recyclables.

United States Environmental Protection Agency
Office of Solid Waste
401 M St., SW
Washington, DC 20460
EPA Solid Waste Hot Line:
(800) 424-9346
Or contact the regional EPA branch nearest to where you live.

Whirlpool Corp.
Paper Recycling Program Administrator
Mail Drop #2801
Benton Harbor, MI 49022

Further Reading

Other *How on Earth* books published by The Millbrook Press:

How on Earth Do We Recycle Glass? by Joanna Randolph Rott and Seli Groves.

How on Earth Do We Recycle Metal? by Rudy Kouhoupt with Donald B. Marti, Jr.

How on Earth Do We Recycle Plastic? by Janet Potter D'Amato with Laura Stephenson Carter.

Buy Now, Pay Later! Smart Shopping Counts by Thompson Yardley (Brookfield, CT: The Millbrook Press, 1992).

Garbage! Where It Comes From, Where It Goes by Evan & Janet Hadingham (New York: Simon & Schuster, 1990).

A Kid's Guide to How to Save the Planet by Billy Goodman (New York: Avon Books, 1990).

Paper by Elizabeth Simpson Smith (New York: Walker and Company, 1984).

Recycling Paper by Judith Condon (New York, Franklin Watts, 1991).

Re-Uses: 2,133 Ways to Recycle and Reuse the Things You Ordinarily Throw Away by Carolyn Jabs (New York: Crown Publishers, 1982).

What a Load of Trash! Rescue Your Household Waste by Steve Skidmore (Brookfield, CT: The Millbrook Press, 1991).

INDEX

ABOUT THE AUTHORS

Helen Jill Fletcher has written on a wide variety of how-to subjects that stimulate young people's interests and creativity. She is the author of 125 children's books. As a former teacher and early childhood education specialist, she has edited many books for children and contributed her expertise to magazines and radio and television productions.

She lives in New York City.

Seli Groves, a journalist and syndicated columnist, has created and edited juvenile magazines and written several books. She has always been an active supporter of environmental groups and views recycling as one of our most important and exciting challenges as we rapidly approach the twenty-first century.

She is a member of the American Society of Journalists & Authors, New York Academy of Sciences, and the Society of Children's Book Writers. She is a resident of New York City.